TO THE ONES I LOVE

You are my INSPIRATION, GUIDES, TEACHERS, LAUGHTER,
and most of all MY LOVE.

TIPPIE - From the MOMENT, I held you in my arms,
I knew a STAR was born.

DAISY - You are WATER that brings LIFE to a tree in the DESERT.

SPIRIT - You are my TEACHER, my INSPIRATION for hope.
With YOU, anything is POSSIBLE.

NALA - My SWEETEST little girl. You are the LIGHT that SHINES in
the darkest of NIGHTS.

JACKSON - My MENTOR, CLOSEST FRIEND, and CONFIDENT.

I CHERISH every waking MOMENT with you ALL.
MOM

Author

Nyx Nightshade is a mom, entrepreneur, energy healer, and published author. Her animals and actual live events inspire her books. She is certified in Reiki, Blue Stone & Crystal Healing. She lives in Toronto, Ontario, with her horses and donkeys.

Illustrator

Andre Vitali is an internationally acclaimed illustrator / graphic designer who has lived and worked in Italy and Ireland. Andre began developing his drawing skills as a child. He Graduated in 2005 from L' Accademia Delle Belle Arti University. He lives in Monreale, Italy.

Narrator

Angela Clark is a voice artist. She has enjoyed voicing many different genres and thoroughly enjoys every aspect of voice-over. However, audiobook narration was her starting point. She always enjoyed reading, so audiobook narration was a natural progression of that passion.
She's had the privilege of working directly with several different publishers and many authors.
Angela has narrated over 150 audiobooks and over 200 hours of audio dramas.

STAY CONNECTED!

Tippie-Doo's website at www.tippie-doo.com

  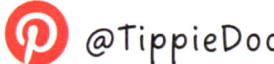

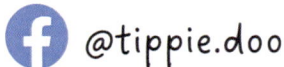 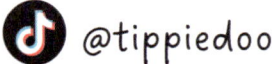 

Scan the QR code to access the digital version of the book.

It is fully narrated in the children's voices by Angela Clark
and illustrated by Andre Vitali.

www.tippie-doo.com

DR. TIPPIE

BY NYX NIGHTSHADE

ILLUSTRATED BY ANDREA VITALI
NARRATED BY ANGELA CLARK

"Good morning, kids! I hope you had sweet dreams."

"Yay, Mama is here! We get to go out and play in the big field!" yelled Tippie.

"Not before you wash your face and comb your hair. And please, do not come back dirty! Otherwise, I will have to give you another bath," said Mama.

2

"Yuck, a bath! Did you all hear that?" screeched Tippie.

"Yes, little one, a bath," laughed Mama.

"No way! The last time you bathed us, we were so clean that it was nearly impossible to get dirty again.
Our ears are still squeaking!" giggled Tippie.

Mama laughed in response to the look on Tippie's face and replied, "You better hurry before I change my mind, little Tippie."

"Come on, guys, let's have some fun," Tippie waved.

They all hurried out of the gate as quickly as they could. However, Jackson was so excited, that he bucked in the air and cut his hoof along the fence.

"Oh goodness!" said Mama. "Come with me! We must clean and wrap your hoof immediately."

Tippie ran back to see where Jackson was and saw him at the house with Mama.

"Jackson, we all are waiting for you to play!" he shouted.

"I was so excited that I cut my hoof, and now Mama needs to wrap it," said Jackson.
"Let me help you, please!" pleaded Tippie. "I know what to do."

"You certainly can!" replied Mama.

Tippie put on Mama's doctor's coat and excitedly opened the first aid kit. Swinging the stethoscope around his neck, he wrapped a bright light around his head.

Jackson and Mama looked at each other and began to giggle.

10

11

"Now, Jackson, I want you to open your mouth and say Ahhh."

"Tippie, I have a cut on my foot, not a sore throat!" laughed Jackson.

"You can never be too careful. It's best to listen to Dr. Tippie—he knows what's good for you!" he joked.

Jackson opened his mouth and shouted, "Ahhh."

Tippie shined his light and said, "Your teeth are big, your tongue is long, and your gums are pink. Yep, that looks healthy!"

15

"Now, let's listen to your heart," Tippie added. "I want you to stay very quiet and take a deep breath in and out."

"Tippie! What are you doing?" bellowed Jackson.

"I'm trying to count your heartbeat," whispered Tippie.

"You're making my heart beat faster!" screamed Jackson.

"Jackson! You must let me examine you so that we can get down to the real problem," Tippie said firmly.

"Tippie, I mean it! Stop horsing around or I will wrap you up in bandages myself!" roared Jackson.

16

"Dr. Tippie, what is your diagnosis?" Mama asked, trying not to laugh.

"I can tell you that my patient is a grumpy donkey with a cut on his foot. I can take care of it in no time," Tippie said confidently.

"That's what I was trying to tell you in the first place! Please bandage my hoof so that we can play!" Jackson pleaded desperately.

Tippie applied a bandage around Jackson's neck, rolled it over his body, and secured it around his hoof. He pondered how to keep it in place and finally had an idea. He covered Jackson's entire body with yellow band-aids.

Pleased with himself, Tippie then brushed Jackson's hooves and declared proudly, "I'm all done!"

"Tippie, what did you do to me? I look like a giant banana!" Jackson chuckled, forgetting his frustration.

21

Tippie and Mama laughed so loud that Daisy, Nala, and Spirit came running to see what fun they were missing. When they saw Jackson covered in band-aids, they began to laugh hysterically.

"Jackson, you look like a banana! We might have to eat you!"

"I sure do, guys, don't I?" laughed Jackson.
"I feel so much better now."

" Thank you so much, Tippie," Jackson said, hugging him tightly. "You not only fixed my hoof but also made us all laugh. Most importantly, you loved me enough to take care of me. I love you, Tippie Doodle."